The Sun and Its Planets

by Thea Feldman

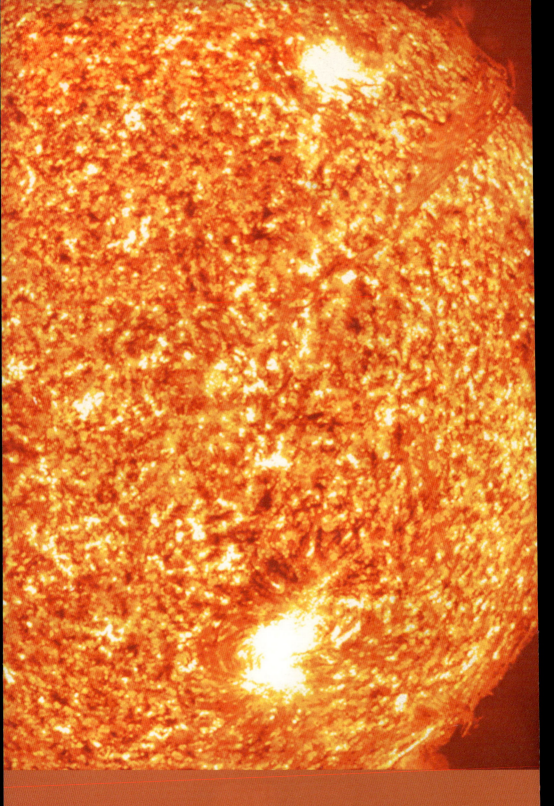

A Giant Star

Did you know that the Sun is actually a star? The Sun and all the other stars in the sky are made up of plasma, or very hot, glowing gases. The Sun is a medium-sized star. It is huge. If the Sun were hollow, one million Earths could fit inside it.

You may start to feel hot when the temperature reaches around 27°C. But the center of the Sun is more than 15,000,000°C! It is hard to imagine how hot that is. Even the surface of the Sun is 5,500°C. No spacecraft can land on the Sun because it's too hot.

We see the Sun only during the daytime. Do you know why? This is because Earth is slowly turning, or rotating around its axis. One rotation takes 24 hours. It's daytime when your part of Earth is facing the Sun.

Axis

The part of Earth that faces the Sun experiences daytime. The part that faces away from the Sun experiences nighttime.

The Solar System

Earth rotates every 24 hours. It also moves around the Sun while it is rotating. The Sun's gravity keeps Earth moving in a path, or orbit, around it.

Earth travels in a slightly oval-shaped orbit around the Sun. One complete orbit takes 365 days and 6 hours. We call this period of time a year. It is amazing to think that Earth is constantly orbiting and rotating and we never feel a thing!

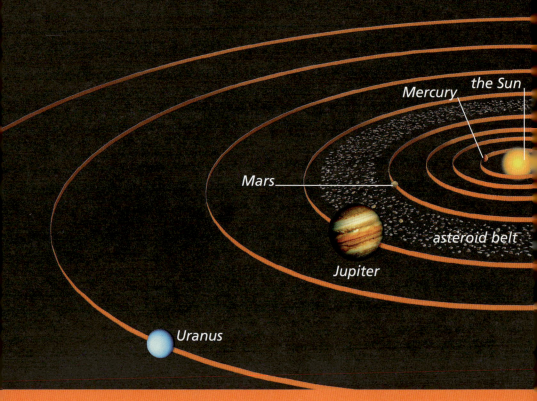

Other objects move around the Sun too. A planet is a large body that orbits around the Sun. Ancient Greeks thought the planets were wandering stars. That is why they named them "planetes," which means wanderers.

There are eight planets that orbit the Sun. Asteroids, or chunks of rock, also orbit the Sun. Everything is held in place by the Sun's gravitational pull. The Sun, the planets and their moons, dwarf planets, and asteroids make up the solar system.

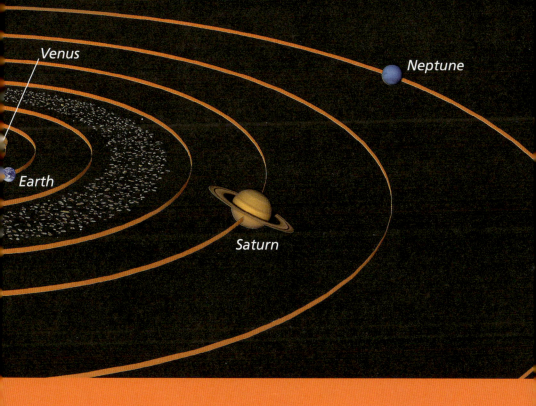

The Planets

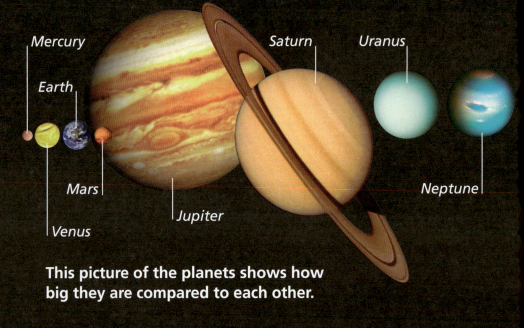

This picture of the planets shows how big they are compared to each other.

The Inner Planets: Mercury

Each of the nine planets is different. They are divided into two main groups: the inner and the outer planets. The inner planets are Mercury, Venus, Earth, and Mars. They are closer to the Sun and have rocky surfaces.

Mercury is the closest planet to the Sun. It takes Mercury only 88 Earth days to make one complete orbit around the Sun. Mercury gets extremely hot during the day. Temperatures there can reach more than 400°C.

But Mercury also gets extremely cold at night. Temperatures can drop lower than −180°C. Antarctica is the coldest place on Earth. Temperatures there drop to only −89°C! The temperatures vary more on Mercury than on any other planet. Mercury is the smallest planet. It is very dry and does not have any atmosphere. It has many craters, just like those found on our Moon. One of Mercury's craters is about 1,300 kilometers (km) across. It is one of the largest craters in the solar system.

Venus

Venus is the second-closest planet to the Sun. It takes 225 days to complete one orbit because it moves very slowly. Venus has the longest day of any planet. It takes 243 Earth days for Venus to rotate just once. Like Mercury, it is very hot and has many craters. Venus, however, has an atmosphere. A thick cloud cover traps heat on Venus. It can be even hotter than Mercury, reaching temperatures of 480°C. The surface of this planet also has volcanoes and lava fields. Venus does not have a moon.

Earth

Earth is the third planet from the Sun, about 150,000,000 km away. It seems to be just the right distance from the Sun to support living things. It is the only planet where water is found in liquid form. Earth also has the mild temperatures that living things need to survive. Earth has a single moon. We have explored the Moon and found that nothing lives there.

The Moon orbits Earth.

Mars

If you look at a photo of the planets from space, Earth looks like a big blue marble. Mars looks like a reddish-orange one. Mars is often called the "red planet." This is because its surface is made of red clay. Most of the surface is rough and dusty, with craters and canyons. The solar system's largest canyon system is on Mars. It stretches about 4,000 km. Mars also has the largest volcano in the solar system. The volcano is now extinct. It is 24 km high and 550 km across. One day on Mars is 25 hours long, about the same as a day on Earth. But one year lasts 687 Earth days. We have sent spacecraft to Mars to see if it ever supported life.

The Outer Planets

The four outer planets are farther away from the Sun than the inner planets. They are very large and are made up mostly of gases. They are often called gas giants. These planets do not have solid surfaces. The atmospheres of the outer planets have thick layers of clouds. They also have rings around them.

There is an asteroid belt that separates the inner and outer planets. While most of the asteroids are very small, some can be as big as 1,000 km across. Many scientists believe these asteroids are all that is left of early planets that collided and broke into pieces.

An asteroid belt separates the inner and outer planets.

The Great Red Spot is a storm of swirling winds.

Jupiter

Jupiter is the first outer planet and the largest planet in the solar system. Jupiter is more than 11 times the size of Earth. It completes a rotation in 10 Earth hours. However, it takes 12 Earth years for Jupiter to orbit the Sun once. It also has more than 60 moons. Most of them are smaller than Earth's moon. The colors of the clouds on Jupiter come from its gases. Winds, clouds, and storms cause the special bands of color. A never-ending storm on the surface of Jupiter is called the Great Red Spot. Jupiter has rings, but they are very hard to see.

Saturn

Saturn is the sixth planet from the Sun. It is also the second largest planet in the solar system. This planet takes 29 Earth years to complete one orbit around the Sun. Saturn is known for its bright rings that are often easy to see. The rings are made of chunks of ice and rock. These chunks can be as small as a grain of sand or as large as a house. Gravity keeps the rings circling the planet. At least 30 moons also surround it. Since Saturn is a gas giant, it is very light for its size.

Uranus

Unlike the rest of the planets, Uranus rotates on its side. It completes one rotation in just 17 hours. Uranus takes 84 Earth years to complete an orbit around the Sun. This seventh planet from the Sun appears bluish-green. It has rings, like Jupiter, but they are very hard to see. Uranus also has at least 26 moons.

Neptune

Neptune is the eighth planet from the Sun. It is about the same size as Uranus, which is four times bigger than Earth. Neptune is similar in color to Uranus. The colors of both Uranus and Neptune come from their planetary gases. Neptune has the strongest winds in the solar system. It orbits the Sun in 165 Earth years and has at least 13 moons.

Pluto

Pluto is a rocky object that orbits far from the Sun. Pluto is very cold, with temperatures dropping lower than –230°C. It is about half the size of Earth's moon.

Pluto has a special orbit. It takes 248 Earth years for Pluto to make one orbit around the Sun. For twenty of those years, Pluto is closer to the Sun than Neptune. Pluto's orbit is at an angle to the orbits of the eight planets.

Until 2006, Pluto was called the ninth planet. Many scientists think that Pluto should never have been called a planet. In August of 2006, scientists decided to put Pluto into a different category. It is now called a dwarf planet.

Huge telescopes collect information about our solar system.

Glossary

asteroids chunks of rock that orbit the Sun

orbit the path that an object, such as a planet or an asteroid, takes as it moves around the Sun

planet a large body that moves around the Sun

solar system the Sun, the nine planets and their moons, and other objects that move around the Sun

What did you learn?

1. What keeps the planets moving around the Sun?

2. What is unusual about the orbit of Pluto?

3. What is Jupiter's Great Red Spot?

4. **Writing in Science** In this book you have read about the inner planets and the outer planets. Write to explain why the outer planets are called gas giants.

5. **Compare and Contrast** Mercury is the first planet. Neptune is the eighth planet. How are these two planets alike? How are they different?

Science Updated

Genre	Comprehension Skill	Text Features	Science Content
Nonfiction	Compare and Contrast	• Captions • Labels • Diagrams • Glossary	Solar System

Scott Foresman Science 3.16

scottforesman.com

ISBN-13: 978-0-328-34232-7
ISBN-10: 0-328-34232-7